Buses, Coaches & Recollections 1959

Midland Red

Contents

Introduction	3
Midland Red Coaches 'out and about'	5
Royal Leamington Spa & Warwick	13
Bus Stops & Stations	17
Inner City Birmingham	23
Suburban Birmingham	31
Out & About Midland Red Town & Country	37
The Leicester Connection	43
1959 Happenings 1	8
1959 Arrivals & Departures	21
1959 Happenings 2	28
1959 TV Favourites a selection	34
1959 No 1 Records	36
1959 Happenings in Sport	46
1959 Happenings 1	47

Series Introduction

The *Recollections Series* is a growing collection of titles providing in an accessible way, a juxtapositioning of photographic illustration of a transport subject with the events, happenings and highlights of a wider sphere and calendar. This series, takes a particular year and place with the views displayed alongside a carefully selected pot-pourri of what happened in that twelve-month period. The vast majority of the images in the first few books were from the Ray Ruffelll collection, held by the publisher, but material from other sources is now being interspersed where felt necessary to maintain appropriate variety. The main criterion for inclusion in these books is for the images to be both interesting and aesthetically pleasing within a chosen theme.

The books are aimed at a more general market than mere transport aficionados or enthusiasts and the authors hope and trust that they will be sure in their aim and that you, the reader, will find much to enjoy, appreciate, enthuse about and even smile about! And it is hoped that some of your own memories are stirred along the way and that you may wish to share these with friends!

First published in 2007
Reprinted 2009

ISBN 978 1 85794 301 6
Silver Link Publishing Ltd
The Trundle
Ringstead Road
Great Addington
Kettering
Northants NN14 4BW

Tel/Fax: 01536 330588
email: sales@nostalgiacollection.com

Website: www.nostalgiacollection.com

British Library Cataloguing in Publication Data
A catalogue record for this book is available from the British Library.
Printed and bound in the Czech Republic

Frontispiece: **SHROPSHIRE** Rural Shropshire is interspersed with a market towns and settlements such as Ironbridge and Coalbrookdale which were the very cradles of the Industrial Revolution. Midland Red, from its garages in Shrewsbury and Wellington, linked these towns and villages with a network of rural bus services usually operated by single-deck buses. One such route was the 909 service and 3599, NHA 599, a Metro-Cammell-bodied BMMO S10 is travelling towards Wellington from Kidderminster on the A442. The conductor standing on the platform next to the driver probably had the best view of the countryside as it flashed by.
R. F. Mack

Opposite background: **STREETLEY** Waiting at the Foley Road East terminus of the 101 route at Streetly Station is 4124, THA 124. This 1954-vintage BMMO D7 had a Metro-Cammell H32/26R body which was of fairly lightweight construction, weighing about 7 tons 2 cwt. Coupled with the improved KL type 8.028 litre engine, meant that the D7 could cope with both town routes and longer inter urban services and have a good turn of speed. Streetly Station opened on 1 July 1879 and was an intermediate station on the circular Birmingham New Street, Sutton Park, Walsall, Bescot and New Street service. Streetly Station closed early in the post-Beeching era in 1965. *R. F. Mack*

Introduction

1959 was a strange year in many ways...

The post-war years of austerity and ration books had gone, but the "Swinging Sixties" had yet to arrive. The Conservative Party was swept back into power in October largely due to the idea laid down two years earlier by Prime Minister Harold Macmillan that "You've never had it so good", but only the well-off could afford to go on holiday abroad. Car ownership was increasing and beginning to affect the success of public transport, while the revolutionary Mini was being offered for £497. Britain's first long stretch of motorway, the M1 was opened in November and it briefly became a tourist attraction to either just watch the cars speeding along the stretch between Rugby and Watford or to drive hell-for-leather along the three lane motorway in these halcyon days before speed limits, central barriers and contemporary cars with lousy brakes!

Television was being transformed by the competition to the BBC from the ITV commercial companies and people were being lured to their firesides to watch new programmes such as Juke Box Jury and Bonanza and away from the cinemas and theatres.

Britain still smelt of boiled cabbage and sprouts every Sunday lunchtime, but the first 'foreign' restaurants were beginning to find favour in the larger cities, though Britain was not the cosmopolitan country that it is today. Many of the large cities and towns were only just beginning to redevelop their urban landscapes after the Second World War so the old "bomb building" site was still a playground for the local children. Slums were being pulled down and being replaced by the Utopian ideals of le Corbusier with cities in the sky.

It was still a sergeant's world but the clouds were on the horizon in 1959. Three years before, the Suez Crisis had proved finally that Britain was no longer the omnipotent colonial power that she had pretended to be for most of the 20th century. Within ten years inexorable industrial decline would have set in, as well as a feeling that everyone was better off in the brave new egalitarian Britain. In 1959, the old order was beginning to fade, new ideas were being formulated and change was in the air.

And so to Midland Red whose claim to fame in 1959 was that it began running express motorway coaches between Birmingham and London using the new M1 motorway. The photographs in the book are credited to the photographers who took the pictures, many of whom are long dead and whilst a genuine attempt has been made to use only photographs which were taken in 1959 a few from late 1958 or early 1960 might have crept in if they were not dated. So dear reader, forgive your humble correspondent if there is a non-1959 photograph but enjoy the nostalgia of the Midlands as served by the Birmingham and Midland Motor Omnibus Company, better known as Midland Red.

David Harvey, Dudley
November 2007,

Below: **DIGBETH COACH STATION**
Originally opened on 3 January 1929, Digbeth garage was also the Birmingham & Midland Motor Omnibuses' primary coach station. For this purpose the front length of Digbeth garage was used as a departure point, entering from Rea Street and leaving from the other end by way of Milk Street. Thirty years later and just one season before withdrawal, 2277, FHA 409, a thirty-seater Duple coach-bodied SOS ONC dating from 1939, loads up in the coach station before leaving on a coach service to Banbury by way of Stratford-upon-Avon.
D. R. Harvey Collection

Above: **DIGBETH COACH STATION**
The 1939 SOS ONC coaches had long and active lives and leaving Digbeth Coach Station via the Mill Street exit in 1959 is 2291, FHA 423. These front engined coaches looked very modern when they were constructed and their Duple designed bodies were echoed in the post-war bodies on the forty-five underfloored BMMO C1 chassied coaches which entered service about ten years later. 2291 is leaving on the regular coach service to Bournemouth.
PM Photography

Midland Red Coaches 'out and about'

Below: **DIGBETH** The BMMO C5 coaches were the first motorway coaches in Britain. The opening of the first section of the M1 between Rugby and Watford enabled Midland Red to implement the first Birmingham to London Motorway express coach service on 2 November 1959. 4809, 809 HHA a brand-new CM5T, the toilet compartment being behind the frosted glass of the nearside rear corner, leaves Digbeth Coach Station a few days after the service to London was begun. *L. Mason*

Above: **CARLYLE ROAD WORKS**
Under construction at Carlyle Road Works in late 1959 is 4814, later to be registered 814 HHA, when the body had been framed and partially panelled. In this state the body can be seen to be heavily based on the framing of the S14 and S15 single-deck buses. It entered serviced in 1960 designated as a CM5T which meant that it was a motorway coach which had 34 seats and a toilet compartment. In this state the one-piece glass-fibre moulded roof had yet to be fitted
D. R. Harvey Collection

Below: **M45 Motorway** A CM5T coach in its natural environment! 4809, 809 HHA is parked ! on the inside lane of the newly opened M45 motorway in late 1959 about the time of the inauguration of the Birmingham to London "Motorway Express" service. These coaches, with their famous leopard spot upholstery, revolutionised coach travel when they first went on the road and it literally took years for the mainstream British coach chassis makers to catch up with Midland Red. Capable of well-over their official top speed of 85 mph, memories of travelling flat out on the M1 in a contemporary car, such as a Standard 10, a Morris Minor or bigger cars such as Ford

Consuls, Vauxhall Victors and Austin A55s, are being overtaken at speed by one of these CM5T coaches. *A. Ingram*

Above: **VICTORIA COACH STATION** Journeys end at Victoria Coach Station on 22 November 1959. This is the prototype CM5 coach, 4722, 722 BHA, which was probably going to be the last of the S14 single-deckers but was built up as a 37-seater C5 coach in 1958. Originally it had a deep two-piece curved windscreen but in 1959 this was replaced with a very individualistic "Midland Red" solution to the problems of reflection from the lower saloon lights at night. The Dutch bus style of "lantern" multi-faceted windscreen was adopted for 4722 and became the standard for the production vehicles. *M. A. Sutcliffe*

Left: **GRETNA GREEN** The BMMO C2 class of coaches were designed with Duple C26C bodies especially for touring or as Midland Red called them "Coach Cruises". The last of the class, 3356, KHA 356, was one of three of the class of ten which were given a face lift for the 1959 season which involved giving them a new radiator grill and a full width front bumper. 3356 is waiting in front of the Old Blacksmith's Shop at Gretna Green on a "Scottish Cruise" *A. D. Broughall*

Below: **CHELTENHAM** In the 1959 season, ten 1939 SOS ONC coaches were lent to Black & White Motorways in Cheltenham. Five of them are waiting for customers in Cheltenham Coach Station in June of that year. The nearest coach is 2286, FHA 418, which was retained for special events after the rest of the class were taken out of service in 1960. It did seem a jinx vehicle, as in both May 1961 and 1963 it carried the players of Leicester City F.C. who on both occasions were the defeated FA Cup finalists. In 1964 this sole surviving ONC was bought for preservation but even that was doomed as the preservationists could not keep their coach due to the lack of a suitable storage site. *M. A. Sutcliffe*

1959 Happenings 1

January
• Alec Guinness knighted in new Years Honours List.
• General de Gaulle inaugurated as First President of the Fifth French Republic.
• Worst winter fog in London since 1952.
• 11 year old Birmingham schoolgirl Gail Bradley breaks World record by spinning a hula-hoop for 17 minutes.
• Henry Cooper outpoints Brian London over 15 rounds to become British and Empire Heavyweight boxing champion.

February
• London Transport unveils plans for new Victoria Underground line from Victoria to Walthamstow at a cost of £50 million.
• Archbishop Makarios arrives in London for talks on Cyprus with Premier Harold Macmillan.
• Harold Macmillan arrives in Moscow for talks with Nikita Khrushchev.

March
• Hawaii approved for 50th state of USA.
• EOKA accepts London agreement over Cyprus.
• Madagascar hurricane kills 3,300 people.

Below: **BAWTRY** Bawtry in South Yorkshire, standing on the River Idle had been an important port before the 12th century but gradually the quays silted up. By the 18th century stage it had become an important coaching change over point along the old Great North Road route. After the 1930s, the wide main street served as a parking point for coaches, coming from all directions carrying passengers wanting refreshments in the town's pubs and restaurants. Standing in front of Bawtry's Working Men's Club on a typically anonymous Midland Red coach tour and alongside an impressive looking Jaguar Mk VII, is 3349, KHA 349. By 1959 this BMMO C2 coach with a Duple body had been reseated by four to C30C putting them in line with the larger batch of C1s. *D. R. Harvey Collection*

Below: **CHEDDAR** One of the most popular day tours was to Cheddar Gorge in Somerset. A run down in the pre-motorway days to Gloucester for a cup of tea was followed by another hours drive to Axbridge to look at King John's Hunting Lodge before arriving at the village of Cheddar. BMMO C1s, 3338, KHA 338 and 3304, KHA 304, have climbed out of the steepest part of Cheddar's magnificent Jurassic limestone gorge which was carved out by melt-water from a nearby ablating ice sheet in an interglacial during the recent Pleistocene Period. I can't imagine that the driver knew that! *A. A. Cooper*

Below: **GREAT YARMOUTH** In August 1959 in the Eastern Counties Coach Station in Great Yarmouth, a fairly rare event occurred as parked alongside each other were four Midland Red coaches each representing a different period of Midland Red coaches. Unfortunately they are not parked in chronological order, but on the left is 3307, KHA 307, a Duple-bodied underfloor engined coach which went on the road in 1949. Overnight, this class of coach made every other operator's vehicles look obsolete! Next to it is the newest coach of the quartet; 4793, 793 GHA, is a brand new 37 seater C5, while on its right is the oldest of the coaches. This is 2272, FHA 404, a 1939 Duple-bodied SOS ONC which had been withdrawn in 1958 and then returned to service for another two summers before succumbing again at the end of the 1960. Finally on the right is Willowbrook-bodied C3 coach 4232, UHA 232, of 1954. In 1962, 4232 was one of sixteen of the batch which were transformed by being rebodied with Plaxton "Panorama" C36F bodies which were 32' 6" long and 8' 2" wide. They were the only modern Midland Red coaches to be rebodied. *M. A. Sutcliffe*

Right: **LONDON** The C3s and C4s were the last BMMO single-deckers built with a chassis and were substantial looking machines. The C3s had bodies built by Willowbrook to the designs of Midland Red and while not suited to the motorway work introduced five years after their construction, they were ideal for excursions and day trips. 4238, UHA 238 finds itself on one such duty and is parked near London Bridge Station in company with a Vauxhall Velox and an Austin A35 saloon. *M. Rooum*

Below: **NORTHAMPTON** The third batch of post-war coaches was the 30' long by 8" wide BMMO C3s. They were fitted with Willowbrook C37C bodies which weighed around 7 tons. There were sixty-three of these attractive but heavyweight coaches which entered service for the 1954 season. 4201, UHA 201, stands in Derngate Coach Station, Northampton while taking a break on its way to Coventry. Behind is a Royal Blue Bristol LS6B with an ECW coach body with unusually by this time, a roof luggage rack. *R. F. Mack*

Below: **BOURNEMOUTH** Midland Red undertook coach excursions to Weston-Super-Mare, Llandudno, Aberystwyth, Skegness, Great Yarmouth, Torquay, Blackpool and Bournemouth as well as having daily services to these resorts. 4219, UHA 219, a BMMO C3 of 1954 is working on the Bournemouth service C during the 1959 season, which left Digbeth at 9:30 am and arrived at the Royal Blue Coach Station in the Square at 6:05 pm, journey time of 8 hours and 35 minutes in these pre-motorway days. *D. R. Harvey Collection*

Upper left: LEAMINGTON SPA A line up of buses which any enthusiast would die for! Midland Red buses loaded up in Old Warwick Road in front of the former GWR Leamington Spa General Station and just up the road from the Midland Red Leamington bus garage towards the southern edge the town centre. 4757, 757 BHA, a 1957 BMMO D7 is sandwiched between a pair of SOS FEDDs with at the tail of the queue 2123, EHA 255, dating from 1938 while at the far end is 2228, FHA 210, a similar Brush forward entrance double-decker but which was a year newer.
P. Kingston

Lower left: LEAMINGTON SPA
Leamington Spa general Station is on the site of the first through station in the town, opened by the GWR on its new line from Birmingham to Oxford in 1852. The present Art-Deco station dates from its comprehensive rebuilding between 1937 and 1939 and has four platforms. Standing outside the station forecourt is a very early post-war single-decker; one of only three to have entered service in 1946. 3006, HHA 607, a BMMO S6 with a lengthened Metro-Cammell B44F body is working on the L44 route to Emscote and Warwick and survived until 1963. Drawn up behind the S6 is 4584, 584 AHA, an integrally constructed BMMO S14 which would be converted to OMO in 1961. *P. Kingston*

1851, the L&NWR opened another branch from Rugby, but only opened its own station alongside the GWR station in February 1854. The L&NWR's new station, with its entrance off Avenue Road, was called "Leamington Avenue". Despite their proximity, the two railways in Leamington remained separate and it was not until 1908 that a junction was constructed for passenger trains. This allowed L&NWR trains from the Rugby direction to use the GWR station which became known as "Leamington Spa General". Standing outside the Victorian station buildings is 3731, NHA 731, a 1950 BMMO S10 chassis with the last body ever built by Brush for Midland Red to the original 27' 6" length, albeit lengthened in 1950 to 30' 0". This vehicle survived until 1965. *P. J. Yeomans*

Above: **LEAMINGTON SPA** Working on the X57 service, 3291, JHA 891, stands in front of the hoardings in Old Warwick Road on 27 March 1959. This BMMO S8 with a Metro-Cammell B44F body belonged to the first class of one hundred 8' wide single-deckers. By this time, spray painting had reduced the Midland bus fleet to an all over red livery which was a pity as the fleet looked far better with black-painted wings and gold lining out. Alas, the era of economic cut backs had begun and this was just the first of many measures which gradually permeated the bus industry *P. Kingston*

Right: **LEAMINGTON SPA** The L&NWR reached Leamington in December 1844, with a branch from Coventry built by the London and Birmingham Railway. That line terminated at New Milverton, and the L&NWR did not open a more central station until 1854. In March

Right: **LEAMINGTON SPA** Parked in George Street, Leamington Spa near to Radford Road and within a bus stop of High Street in May 1959 is BMMO S8 3255, JHA 855. This 8' wide MCCW forty-four seater had been extended by Roe from 27' 6" to 30' which can be seen by the extra long rear side saloon window and the extra panelling. Waiting alongside the Regency terraced houses is FHA 423, a 1939 Duple-bodied SOS ONC which was being used on a bus service to Wellesbourne.
P. Kingston

Left: **LEAMINGTON SPA** A study of rear ends. Standing on the open hard standing at Myton Road garage in May 1959 is 3082, HHA 683, a 1947 BMMO S6 single-decker with a Brush body. The earlier postwar Midland Red single-deckers had, like 3082, both a rear number and destination box though by 1948 this arrangement was replaced by a single number box. The Leamington Spa Myton Road garage was opened in September 1957 which explains why the buildings look so pristine. The integral-construction BMMO S14 on the left is 4332, UHA 332, which was at this time only three years old. *P. Kingston*

variable rubber suspension were all combined in a 30' long double-decker which had a capacity for 72 passengers. And all this for 8 tons 2 cwts! *A. B. Cross*

Below: **COVENTRY** Passengers are rushing to board the single-decker which is about to leave Pool Meadow bus station in 1959. 3229, JHA 829, a 1948-built BMMO S8 with an MCCW B44F body, stands in the old Pool Meadow Bus Station when working on the 567 service to Leamington Spa via Cubbington and Stoneleigh. Pool Meadow bus station had opened in October 1931 and was used for coach services, coach tours as well as the many stage carriage services of Midland Red and of course City of Coventry Corporation, one of whose Daimler CVA6 is manoeuvring behind the Midland Red single-decker.
D. G. Savage

Above: **STRATFORD UPON AVON** The prototype BMMO D9, 4773, 773 KHA, stands at the Red Lion bus station at The Bridge in Stratford-upon-Avon about one year after entering service. It is about to return to Birmingham on the long 150 service via Henley-in-Arden and Shirley. Although the rather ordinary Carlyle bodywork looks little more than a stretched D7, this bus was really advanced. The reason why the D9 double-decker was so radical was not because any single item was particularly innovative, but it was that they all appeared on one vehicle and unlike on the Guy "Wulfrunian" nearly everything worked! A large 10.45 BMMO KL engine was coupled to a Self Changing gearbox while power steering, independent front suspension, a short 17' 1" wheelbase and

Below: **LEICESTER** In June 1959, 3483, MHA 483, is parked in St Margaret's Bus Station, Leicester between turns on the L8 service to South Wigston. This Brush-bodied D5 belonged to the last class of open platform double-deckers to be built for Midland Red. Indeed other than the six double-decker buses taken over from *Kemp & Shaw* of Leicester on New Years Day 1959, there were only the two batches of AD2 AEC "Regent" IIs, the GD6 Guy-bodied Guy "Arab" IIIs and the D5s which didn't have rear platform doors. 3483 was unusual as it had extra ventilation intakes in its front dome and as late as June 1959 had yet to have the top of the windscreen raised, as taller drivers complained about the limited forward visibility and sore necks! *G. H. F. Atkins courtesy J. Banks*

Above: **WORCESTER** On a bright summer's day in 1959 the second of the initial batch of S14 single-deckers, 4255, UHA 255, stands in Worcester Bus Station in Newport Street. The bus is working on the 387 route along the Vale of Evesham alongside the River Avon back through Evesham by way of Pershore. The S14 single-decker perhaps looked plain but under the skin it was a ground-breaking design. Weighing just over an amazingly light 5 tons, they were chassis-less, had disc brakes on all wheels and had independent front suspension utilising rubber springing on both axles. Extensive use was made of glass fibre with an all-in-one moulded roof and with the BMMO KL 8.028 litre engine, it could carry 44 people. The bodies on these lightweight buses did however shake badly on indifferent road surfaces. 4255 lasted until 1970 giving it an operational life of fifteen years. *D. G. John*

Below: **STOURBRIDGE** Many of the Stourbridge local bus services terminated on the forecourt of Stourbridge Town railway station. This station next to Foster Street was opened by the Great Western Railway on 1 October 1879 on the short spur from the Junction Station. This line is just less than one mile long and is the shortest branch line in Britain. A pair of Brush-bodied AEC "Regent" IIs stand on the station forecourt. 3111, JHA 12 is working on the S50 which had a 10 minute journey time to High Park Estate while 3109, JHA 10, is allocated to the S56 route to the Norton Estate. *J. Tenpent*

Above: **HEREFORD** Waiting for both passengers and crew in Hereford Bus Station with the Odeon Cinema in the background, is 3010, HHA 611, a 44 seat Metro-Cammell bodied S6 which had entered service in early 1947. It had been lengthened to 30' long by Roe in 1953. The MCCW bodies on the S6s could be best identified from the Brush-bodied buses by their destination boxes having a more sloping corner profile and slightly higher mounted front side lights. The S6 is working on the H8 City service to Brockhampton which is half way to Ross-on-Wye. *J. S. Smith*

Below: **WELLINGTON** 3633, NHA 633 is parked at the Charlton Street bus shelter located next to Wellington's bus garage. This garage had been opened in September 1953 and replaced an earlier garage. This Metro-Cammell-bodied BMMO S10 is working on the W40 which was a Wellington Town service. This bus entered service in 1950 and was quite an early withdrawal, being taken out of service in 1963. *M. J. Bray*

Below: **EVESHAM** Having just loading up, S14 single-decker 4707, 707 BHA, is standing in Evesham's wide High Street which also served as a bus station. Originally this was part of the

Above: **NUNEATON** 3217, JHA 817, stands in Nuneaton bus station alongside JXC 200. This double-decker had formerly been London Transport's RT 1437 and which had been sold early because of its non-standard Craven body, via Bird's of Stratford to Lloyds of Nuneaton. The Midland Red S8's Metro-Cammell-body had been rebuilt by

Willowbrook in 1958 with an S15 front and power doors, was one of three of the class to receive this modification which certainly updated their appearance. The three rebuilt single-deckers were reclassified S8 Mark I but this hardly lengthened their lives, with 3217 being withdrawn as early as 1962 *D. R. Harvey Collection*

A46 between Stratford and Cheltenham but in recent times has had its traffic problems alleviated by a by-pass. 4707 is working on the 402 circular route and is about to lave from its loading up point in front of the Star public house. On the left is a 1952 Norfolk registered Standard Vanguard Phase I car. *R. Marshall*

1959 Arrivals & Departures

Births

John McEnroe	Tennis player	16 February
Emma Thompson	Actress	15 April
Sheena Easton	Singer	27 April
Ben Elton	Actor, Novelist, Playwrite	3 May
Kevin Spacey	Actor	26 July
Gerhard Berger	Racing Driver	27 August
Lenny Henry	Comedian	29 August
Brian Adams	Author	5 November
Nick Park	Animator	6 December

Deaths

Cecil Blount de Mille	US Film Director	b.1881	21 January
Mike Hawthorn	Racing Driver	b.1929	22 January
Buddy Holly	Singer	b.1936	3 February
Dr.Daniel Malan	SA Prime Minister	b.1874	7 February
Lou Costello	US Comedian	b.1906	3 March
Raymond Chandler	Writer	b.1888	26 March
Frank Lloyd Wright	Architect	b.1869	9 April
John Foster Dulles	US Secretary of State	b.1888	24 May
Billie Holiday	Singer	b.1915	17 July
Sir Jacob Epstein	Sculptor	b.1880	19 August
Gerrard Hoffnung	Humorist/musician	b.1925	28 September
Mario Lanza	Singer	b.1921	7 October
Errol Flynn	Actor	b.1909	14 October
Albert Ketelbey	Composer	b. 1875	26 November

other claim to fame was a deep ford over the River Blythe. This service only operated on Tuesdays, Fridays, Saturdays and Sundays with two buses per day in each direction while on Thursdays there was a third journey. Coming up the steep hill into the Bull Ring is BCT 2587, JOJ 587 a 1950 Guy "Arab" III Special which is coming into Birmingham on a 44A service from Acocks Green. *R. F. Mack*

Below: **BIRMINGHAM** Travelling along the remains of Dudley Street with the soon to be demolished Sydenham Hotel above the S14 single-decker 4573, 573 AHA is 2336, FHA 840. The old hotel had an Atkinson's

Above: **BIRMINGHAM** Midland Red had used a terminus outside St Martin's Parish Church in the Bull Ring since about the end of the First World War. Buses using the area were usually going to Coventry, Stratford or Warwick and 7' 6" wide S6, 3075, HHA 676, is no exception. It is being used on the 186 route. This service went via Hall Green, Solihull and Knowle before reaching the Bull's Head pub at Barston, a small hamlet whose

owned public house on the ground floor; it is dwarfed by the S &U building in Edgbaston Street,. Leading the way along Dudley Street and passing one of Christopher Bryant's construction workers huts is SOS FEDD 2336, FHA 840. This elderly double-decker is travelling towards Station Street on a Bank Holiday in the summer of 1959 where it will load up on the 198 service to Tamworth via Curdworth and, even then, Drayton Manor Park. *R. F. Mack*

Below: **BIRMINGHAM** Just beginning the long journey on the 144 service to Worcester and Malvern Wells is SOS FEDD 2346, FHA 850. It is travelling along Hinckley Street with behind it some of the earliest areas to

be demolished in the first stage of the Inner Ring Road scheme which had begun in 1958. 2346 had the usual pre-war Brush front entrance 56 seat body and had entered service in 1939. Even in its final full year of service it was still being employed on all-day front line duties. *R. F. Mack*

Above: **BIRMINGHAM** The impressive Station Street cast-iron shelters alongside the southern wall of New Street Station were the preserve of Birmingham Corporation trams, buses and between 1934 and 1951 the Coventry Road trolleybuses. This left the Worcester Street end of Station Street beyond Dudley Street to the tender mercies of Midland Red. BMMO S9 3364, LHA 364, fitted with a Brush B44F body waits for its driver and conductor to come back from having their mug of tea before going back as a 108 service to Sutton Coldfield by way of Erdington and Wylde Green. *R. F. Mack*

Below: **BIRMINGHAM** Coming into Birmingham at the bottom of Camp Hill, with Bordesley station railway bridge in the background, is 2372, FHA 876, a 1939 SOS FEDD with a Brush body. Even at the end of their lives the elderly FEDDs were worked hard on front-line duties. 2372 is working on the 153 route from the Monkspath terminus beyond Shirley at Cranford Avenue. This was one of the numerous and intensive Midland Red routes which serviced Stratford Road well into the Solihull suburbia which lay beyond the BCT 37 bus terminus at the Hall Green City boundary. Years later this would become the terminus for the WMPTE 90 service. *L. Mason*

Above: **BIRMINGHAM** Quite a number of the 1958 SOS FEDD withdrawals were used until 1960 as Driver Training vehicles. One of these was 2141, EHA 273, a 1938 Brush-bodied example, whose learner driver will almost have certainly just done a double-declutch change into first gear on the steep part of Hill Street. With the impressive Birmingham Town Hall facing him, the driver is hauling his twenty-one year old double-decker into Paradise Street as he starts the journey back to Bearwood garage where the driving school was located. *R .F. Mack*

Below: **BIRMINGHAM** Climbing up Summer Hill having just passed the three storied Shakespeare public house on the corner of Lionel Street, is 3788, NHA 788. This BMMO D5B, fitted with an attractive if somewhat solid Brush H30/26RD body, is being employed on the B85 route. This was one of the former B & M tram services which on the expiry of the leases in 1928 were operated by Corporation trams until the "Track" group of services were closed just three weeks into World War II on 30 September 1939. The B85 from Spon Lane was nominally a joint service with BCT though in reality nearly all the duties were operated by Midland Red's Oldbury garage, though an hourly night service was operated by BCT. *R. F. Mack*

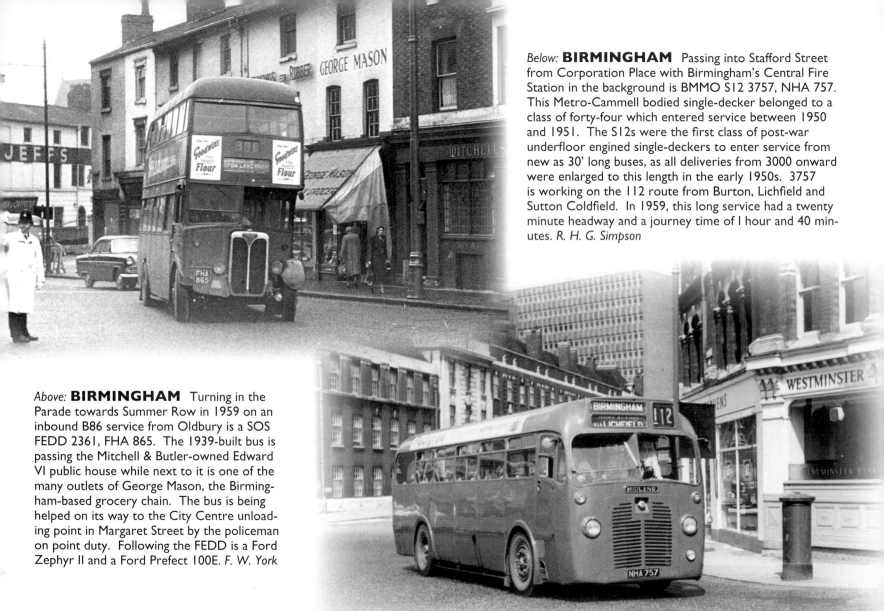

Below: **BIRMINGHAM** Passing into Stafford Street from Corporation Place with Birmingham's Central Fire Station in the background is BMMO S12 3757, NHA 757. This Metro-Cammell bodied single-decker belonged to a class of forty-four which entered service between 1950 and 1951. The S12s were the first class of post-war underfloor engined single-deckers to enter service from new as 30' long buses, as all deliveries from 3000 onward were enlarged to this length in the early 1950s. 3757 is working on the 112 route from Burton, Lichfield and Sutton Coldfield. In 1959, this long service had a twenty minute headway and a journey time of 1 hour and 40 minutes. *R. H. G. Simpson*

Above: **BIRMINGHAM** Turning in the Parade towards Summer Row in 1959 on an inbound B86 service from Oldbury is a SOS FEDD 2361, FHA 865. The 1939-built bus is passing the Mitchell & Butler-owned Edward VI public house while next to it is one of the many outlets of George Mason, the Birmingham-based grocery chain. The bus is being helped on its way to the City Centre unloading point in Margaret Street by the policeman on point duty. Following the FEDD is a Ford Zephyr II and a Ford Prefect 100E. *F. W. York*

Below: **BIRMINGHAM** The learner driver gives a long forgotten hand signal as he turns right out of John Bright Street and into Holloway Head. The driver has learnt the ancient art of giving hand signals as none of the prewar Midland Red buses were fitted with directional indicators. 2243, FHA 225, entered service in early 1939 and was taken out of PSV service in 1957 whereupon it served as a driver training vehicle, or as they were known locally at the time as a "learner bus", until 1961. The "Access To Frontagers Only" sign is an indication that Smallbrook Street has been closed as part of the first stager in the construction of Birmingham's new Inner Ring Road. *F. W. York*

1959
Happenings 2

April
• David Niven, for Best Actor and Wendy Hiller, for Best Supporting Actress both in "Separate Tables" win Oscars.
• Winston Churchill, 85 announces that he will stand for Parliament at next Election.
• Work on St Lawrence Seaway ends after five years.
• Building of Christopher Cockerell's revolutionary hovercraft begins at Saunders-Roe.
• Dalai Llama reaches safety in India.
• NASA chooses 7 test pilots for Mercury Space Programme; they are Scott Carpenter, Gordon Cooper, John Glenn, Virgil Grissom, Walter Schirra, Alan Shephard and Donald Slayton.

May
• British Railways has plans to close 230 railway stations.
• USSR Census shows a total population of 208, 800, 000 people.
• Donald Campbell sets a new water speed record of 260.35 mph.

June
• The Queen opens NATO conference.
• Brigitte Bardot marries Jacques Charrier in Paris.

Upper left: **BIRMINGHAM** Passing through Victoria Square in Birmingham with the begrimed Council House serving as a backdrop is one of the originally magnificent Guy "Arab" IIIs which by 1959 had been re-engined with a BMMO 'K'-type engine. When new, with their Meadows 6DC 10.35 litre engines, they could tackle Castle Hill in Dudley from a standing start with a full load in top gear! It is working on the 140 service back to Dudley by way of Blackheath and Rowley Regis. *F. W. York*

Lower left: **BIRMINGHAM** Standing at the Worcester end of Station Street is 4621, 621 AHA, a 1957 BMMO S15 dual-purpose single-decker. It is waiting at the 112 bus shelter and will shortly leave on the 1 hour 40 minute journey to Burton-upon-Trent. These forty-seaters were intended for use on Midland Red's long distant stage carriage services and were a development of the lightweight S14 buses. They had twin rear wheels, deep cushioned seats, upgraded mechanical details and nearly became a standard single-decker for the BET group. *S. N. J. White*

Below left: **BIRMINGHAM** The Cape Hill, Smethwick, Bearwood, Oldbury and Dudley services were originally tram services operated latterly by Birmingham's municipal trams operating from Rosebery Street depot. Although all the Dudley Road trams except for the 32 route to Lodge Road and the 33 route to Ladywood were withdrawn on 30 September 1939, the cobbles in Edmund Street alongside the tram tracks were still being used by buses as they loaded up at the substantial former tram bus shelters. Standing under the Roman-styled triumphal bridge, built in 1912 to link the City Art Gallery and Museum completed in 1885 to the Council House Extension is BMMO D7 4371, VHA 371, unusually it is working on the Bearwood B82 service which was nearly always operated by Birmingham City Transport. *L. Mason*

Below right: **BIRMINGHAM** Being followed by a 1956 Ford Prefect 100E four-door saloon, 4100, THA 100, a BMMO D7 with a Metro-Cammell body, has turned from Broad Street into Easy Row. When new in late 1953, this bus seated 58 but by 1959 this had been increased to a 63 seater. It is travelling to its Birmingham terminus in the nearby Paradise Street when working on the 140 service from Dudley by way of Blackheath and Bearwood. *F. W. York*

Below: **SALTLEY ROAD** In Saltley Road when working on the 160 service from Coleshill is 4026, SHA 426. This was one of the 100 Leyland "Titan" PD2/12s with Leyland H30/26RD bodies which had entered service in 1953. They were fitted with Leyland's version of the Midland Red concealed radiator for which they borrowed and copied the concealed bonnet assembly of D5B 3876. This was so successful that this front assembly became the standard Leyland option until the early 1960s for a bonneted double-decker bus. *F. W. York*

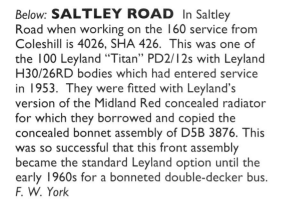

Above: **HALL GREEN** Travelling into Birmingham on a 154 service on the 35 minute service from Solihull to Birmingham is 2231, FHA 213. This bus is a 1939 example of the last flowering of Midland Red's pre-war front-entrance double-decker, thus the designation FEDD. It is in Stratford Road with the junction of Knowle Road on the left where the Austin 8hp car is waiting for the Ford Zodiac to pass. Looking back towards Hall Green, behind the bus is the stone bridge over the River Cole. *F. W. York / A. B. Cross*

Below: **KINGS HEATH** Travelling out of Birmingham in Alcester Road South with the distant Kings Heath Shopping centre in the background is 4609, 609 AHA. It is working on the 343 service which only operated between Mondays and Fridays. There were only two journeys in each direction between Birmingham, the delightful village of Beoley and Redditch. Judging by the long shadows and bright sunlight this S15 dual-purpose single-decker was the 9:05 am departure from All Saint's Parish Church in Kings Heath whose spire can just be made out on the sky-line. *F. W. York / A. B. Cross*

Below: **SELLY OAK** Passing through Selly Oak in July 1959 when travelling into Birmingham along Bristol Road is BMMO S15 4603, 603 AHA. It is working on the 143 service from Bromsgrove, the Lickey Hills and former tram terminus at Rednal. Behind the bus is the old St Mary's School building which was next to the Frederick Road junction. These 40 seat dual-purpose single-deckers had semi-coach accommodation and were better suited to the longer X-lettered cross-country services than the frequent bus route between Birmingham and Bromsgrove. *R. H. G. Simpson*

Above: **HAGLEY ROAD** Speeding along Hagley Road on a 122 service being followed by a Sunbeam 90 Mark III sports saloon is a Brush-bodied SOS FEDD 2343, FHA 847. There were a large number of bus services operated by Midland Red into the Black Country which used the main arterial Hagley Road route and the 122 service was one of them. The 122 was a short working as far as Oldbury of the 120 route to Dudley, but unlike the B86 went "the long way round" by way of Bearwood, the Queen's Head, Londonderry, Langley and then on to Oldbury Bus Station in the shadow of the late Victorian Council House. *A. D. Broughall*

Left: **SMETHWICK** After withdrawal as PSVs, many of the pre-war fleet were put to use as driver training vehicles. Seen in deepest suburban Smethwick is 2427, GHA 348, a 1939-vintage Brush-bodied SOS SON. This 1940-built bus, one of the last half-cab single-deckers to enter service with Midland Red, was withdrawn in 1957 and served as a trainer vehicle until 1961. *A. D. Broughall*

Right: **QUINTON** Passing the Hollybush public house in Hagley Road West, Quinton, Birmingham on 7 July 1959 is 4843, FJF 90, a surprising visitor to the West Midlands. This Guy "Arab" III 5LW with a Barnard B35F body was originally new to *Kemp & Shaw*, Leicester and was taken into the Midland Red fleet on 1 January 1959. Six months later it turned up working on the 40 mile long service to Ludlow! *B. W. Ware*

Below: **ROUNDS GREEN** The BMMO D5 class of one hundred Brush-bodied buses which were the 8' wide equivalent of the wartime D1 prototype double-decker. 3471, MHA 471, was built in 1949 and became one of the last to survive, not being withdrawn until 1965. It is travelling up the steep hill in Taylor's Lane towards the junction with the Wolverhampton Road at Round's Green when working on the 229 service from Bearwood, the nearby Oldbury and over Portway Hill and on to Blackheath. This route was very demanding on the driver's skill as it involved several steep climbs and numerous double-declutch gear changes. *A. D. Broughall*

1959
TV Favourites a selection

World in Action
This hard hitting current affairs programme was first seen in January 1959, and has tackled many controversial topics in succeeding years.

Dr Who
It was during the early evening of Saturday 23 November 1959 that we watched the first ever episode of Dr Who, then played by William Hartnell. The Time Lord's ability to regenerate into various human forms has led to a number of actors playing the part over the years, that latest at the time of writing being David Tennant in the 2007 series.

Ready, Steady, Go!
Almost compulsory Friday evening viewing for teenagers, this show proclaimed 'The Weekend starts here!'

Younger children enjoyed...
Boss Cat, Deputy Dawg and Fireball XL5.

The Dickie Henderson Show was one of the most popular comedy series of 1959.

Our Man at St Mark's was a gentle ecclesiastical comedy, starring Leslie Phillips as a young vicar.

The Marriage Lines starred Richard Briers and Prunella Scales as a newly wed young couple.

Below: **DUDLEY** There have always been a large number of bus services which started in or ran through Dudley. The 244 route started in High Bullen, Wednesbury and arrived in Dudley by way of Great Bridge and Tipton before heading off to Netherton, Old Hill before terminating at Cradley Heath railway station. Thus the route virtually crossed the Black Country from north to south. A.E.C. "Regent" II, 3102, JHA 3, one of the fifty Brush-bodied 56 seaters built in 1948 with the then revolutionary Midland Red style concealed radiator and bonnet assembly, stands in Dudley Bus Station in 1959. The driver is no doubt hoping for a fairly empty bus as these A.E.C.s with their 7.58 litre engines, really struggled for performance on the severe gradients around Dudley. *P. J. Yeomans*

Above: **DUDLEY** Standing at the Pine Road terminus of the D10 route on the Priory Estate on 4 July 1959 is one of the by-now emasculated Guy "Arab" IIIs. 3566, MHA 66, was one of a batch of twenty Guy-bodied buses had been originally fitted with a Meadows 6DC engine especially for the very hilly routes in and around Dudley. The Priory, a 1930s municipal housing estate, had only recently mourned the death on 21 February 1958 of one of the areas most famous sons. Duncan Edwards died at the age of 21 to his injuries received in the Munich air disaster on 6 February. The late Sir Matt Busby said that he "was the best player in the world." *A. J. Douglas*

Below: **WALL HEATH** The 262 route from Dudley travelled though Pensnett and Kingswinford before terminating at Blaze Park, Wall Heath. The driver and conductor stand in front of their charge, 4012, SHA 412, a Leyland "Titan" PD2/12 with a Leyland H30/26R body as it stands outside the Wall Heath Community Centre in Enville Road. This was within a few hundred yards of the Dudley boundary with rural Staffordshire.
A. D. Broughall

1959
No 1 Records

January
   The day the rain came down   *Jane Morgan*
   One night with you   *Elvis Presley*
February
   As I love you   *Shirley Bassey*
March
   Smoke gets in your eyes   *The Platters*
   Side Saddle   *Russ Conway*
April
   It doesn't matter anymore   *Buddy Holly*
May
   A fool such as I / I need your love tonight
                        Elvis Presley
June
   Roulette   *Russ Conway*
July
   Dream Lover   *Bobby Darin*
   Living Doll   *Cliff Richard*
August
   Living Doll   *Cliff Richard*
September
   Only Sixteen   *Craig Douglas*
October
   Here comes summer   *Jerry Keller*
   Mack the knife   *Bobby Darin*
   Travellin light   *Cliff Richard*
November
   Travellin light   *Cliff Richard*
December
   What do you want   *Adam Faith*
   What do you want to make those
   eyes at me for? *Emile Ford & The Checkmates*

Left: **BROMSGROVE - BOURNEHEATH** Despite the destination display of 128 Bearwood, judging by the rural location of this vehicle, it is more than likely that it had been working on the 328 service between Bromsgrove and Bourneheath. The frowning appearance of the upper saloon windows and the wide windscreen are the clues that this bus had been rebuilt in October 1942 as the prototype double-decker to receive a concealed radiator and bonnet assembly. The concealed radiator was removed in 1951 but the other tell-tale remnants of the nine year experiment remained. *A.D.Broughall*

Below: **SOLIHULL LODGE** Midland Red operated a number of Birmingham suburban bus services based around Acocks Green or Marston Green. The 170 route went from the former inside the city boundary via Olton, Grimes Hill, next to Wythall railway station and on to Wythall. This single-decker service is being operated by 3249, JHA 849, a Metro-Cammell-bodied BMMO S8. These vehicles were the first class of 8' wide Midland Red buses and dated from 1948. 3249 was extended to 30' long by Charles Roe which increased the seating capacity by four making it B44F and would be withdrawn in 1962. It is travelling along High Street, Solihull Lodge and is passing the Prince of Wales public house. It is also at the point where the boundaries of Solihull, Bromsgrove and Birmingham intersect. *F. W. York*

Out & About Midland Red Town & Country

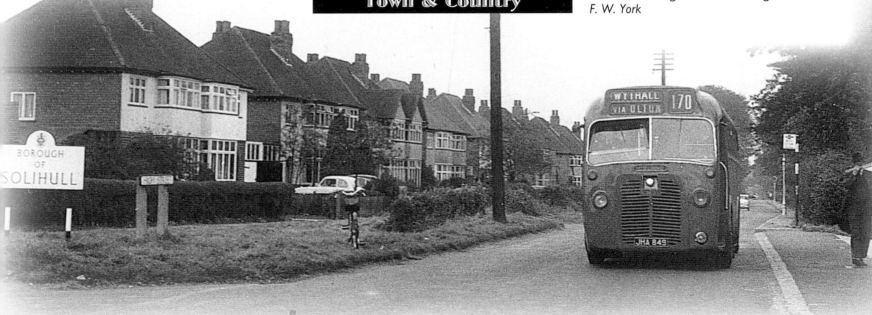

Below: **SOLIHULL LODGE** Today this is a slip road off the A435 between Inkford and the M42. Where the grass bank is located on the right is now part of the dual carriageway going over the lane which starts opposite the Horse & Jockey public house and goes to the top of the steep Weatheroak Hill. In 1959, 3784, NHA 784, a BMMO D5B with a Brush H30/26RD body travels in from Evesham and the nearby village of Portway on the long 148 service into Birmingham. These buses were very solidly built, a tad under-powered, but gave probably the most comfortable ride of all Midland Red's post-war double-deckers.
F. W. York

Below: **CHIPPING CAMPDEN** The 398 service from Evesham had its half-way point on the way to Shipston-on-Stour in the delightful honey-stone buildings of Chipping Campden. BMMO S14 4708, 708 BHA, stands outside the Noel Arms, a 16th century former coaching inn, one of the many welcoming hostelries in the town, while behind it is a rear-engined Renault Dauphine which was extensively advertised in the early days of commercial television with this piece of advertising doggerel: "A penny-farthing a mile, you ride in style, e-c-o-n-o-m-y, the Renault Dauphine." *R. F. Mack*

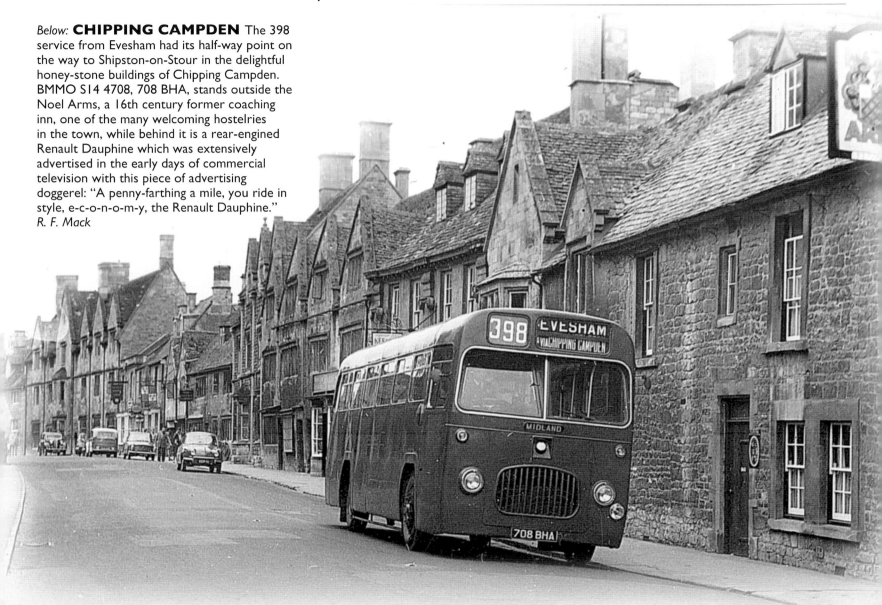

Below: **BANBURY** The last batch of BMMO D7s entered service in 1957 and were the last double-deckers built by Midland Red to have a constant-mesh gearbox. In all there were 350 of these Metro-Cammell-bodied 63-seater D7s built between 1953 and 1957 and they were to be found across the extensive Midland Red operating area. 4748, 748 BHA, is passing into Banbury town centre on a B6 service displaying the helpful TOWN SERVICE and TOWN CENTRE in the destination boxes *PM Photographs*

Below: **BRIDGNORTH** Leaving the High Town part of Bridgnorth along Whitburn Street is 3911, OHA 911, a BMMO S13 with a Nudd Brothers and Lockyer DP40F body which dated from 1952. It is working on one of only three Bridgnorth town services, the B90 route which was operated from Wellington garage and involved the bus coming from Wellington and then doing one town service before heading back to its home town. *PM Photographs*

Above: **IRONBRIDGE** S13 3911, OHA 911, again, but this time the single-decker is travelling through Ironbridge on the 904 service with the World's first iron bridge behind the parked Ford Squire Estate car spanning the River Severn Gorge. The Iron Bridge is the true jewel of Shropshire's Iron-making past and was opened by Abraham Darby III and architect Thomas Pritchard on New Years Day 1781, having been cast from 1779 onwards and it became so famous that now the town proudly boasts the name 'Ironbridge'. Originally the bridge was conceived to allow traffic to cross the Gorge. However, today the bridge is only open to walkers, who wish to stroll across and get a better view of the River Severn.
G. Stainthorpe

Right: **HEREFORD** The Midland Red presence in Hereford consisted of about fifty buses which worked not only the local City services but also on major cross-country services to Ross-on-Wye, Ledbury, Worcester, Leominster and Hay-on-Wye Leaving Hereford bus station on the H2 City service to Westfields and turning into Commercial Road is 3676, NHA 676. This Brush-bodied BMMO S10 dated from 1950 and had been extended to 30' long from 27' 6" by Roe in 1952. Behind the bus is the splendid Art Deco Odeon Cinema. The bus station was for many years the site of Midland Red's Hereford traffic offices.
D. R. Harvey Collection

LEICESTER The driver climbs into the cab of MCCW-bodied S6 single-decker 3001, HHA 602, as passengers prepare to board the 644 service in St Margaret's Bus Station, Leicester. The 644 service went out of Leicester on the Melton Road, A607, to the villages of Gaddesby and Reasby which were both well on the way to Melton Mowbray.
A. D. Broughall

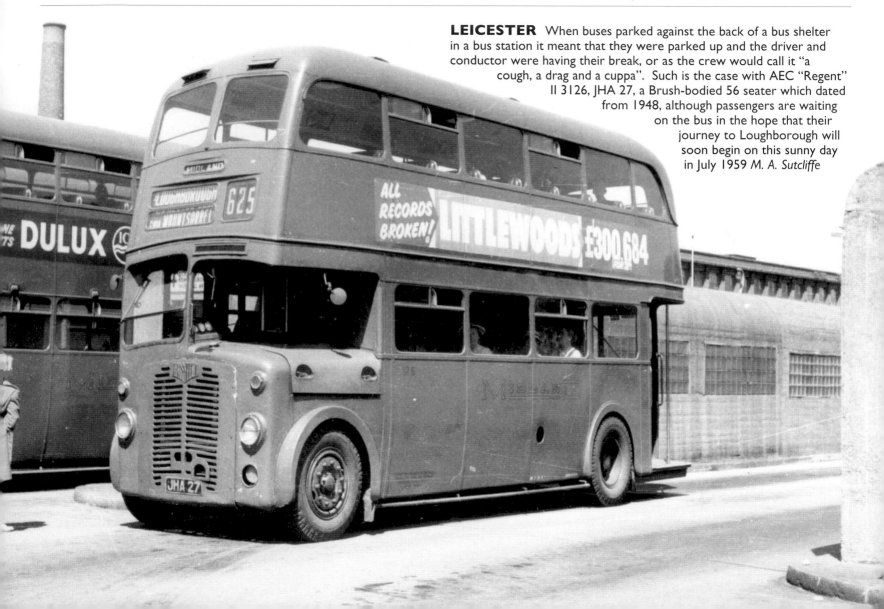

LEICESTER When buses parked against the back of a bus shelter in a bus station it meant that they were parked up and the driver and conductor were having their break, or as the crew would call it "a cough, a drag and a cuppa". Such is the case with AEC "Regent" II 3126, JHA 27, a Brush-bodied 56 seater which dated from 1948, although passengers are waiting on the bus in the hope that their journey to Loughborough will soon begin on this sunny day in July 1959 *M. A. Sutcliffe*

Left: **LEICESTER** Sentinels of Shrewsbury were, like Midland Red, pioneers in the development of underfloor engined single-deckers but did not have the capital to really maintain their early success. Standing in Western Boulevard, Leicester on a Leicester City FC football special on 28 February 1959 is 4847, GUT 543, one of the newly acquired Sentinel STC6s when the fleet of Boyer, Rothley was taken over on 1 February 1959. This one had a Sentinel B44F body which was built to the designs of Beadle who had developed a lightweight single-deck body based on their experience with war-time work with aluminium. *M. A. Sutcliffe*

Right: **LEICESTER** The only lowbridge bus to be operated by Midland Red was *Kemp & Shaw's* 30, GRY 763. This 1950 Leyland "Titan" PD2/1 had a Leyland L27/26R body and once taken over by Midland Red was renumbered 4844. Despite its unusual seating layout 4844 remained in service until 1967. The destination boxes were altered to the standard company style at the main works at Carlyle Road, Edgbaston. It was surprising that the bus was not repainted at the same time in order to get rid of the somewhat unhappy *Kemp & Shaw* livery of brown and pillar box red. The bus is standing at the back of St Margaret's Bus Station in Leicester. *R. Butler*

Above: **LEICESTER** The driver and conductor stand in front of their vehicle miserably looking at the camera and perhaps not regarding the moment as a photograph for posterity but possibly, more prosaically, as their last day of work. It is 31 January 1959 which was the last day of bus operation by Boyer of Rothley. The company would be taken over by Midland Red on 1 February 1959 and three of their vehicles would be taken over. This single-decker, HJU 546, was a Leyland "Royal Tiger" with a Leyland B44F body which had come from Allen of Mountsorrell when that company had also been taken over by Midland Red on the 30 July 1955. *M. A. Sutcliffe*

1959
Happenings in Sport

- Australia win back the Ashes   *5 February*

- OXO wins The Grand National   *21 March*

- Bobby Charlton scores only goal in England's 1-0 defeat of Scotland   *11 April*

- Nottingham Forest beat Luton Town 2-1 in FA Cup Final. Wembley "Jinx" again as goal scorer Roy Dwight breaks leg   *2 May*

- Ingemar Johansson KOs Floyd Patterson in 3rd round to become new World Heavyweight Champion. Patterson is knocked down seven times!   *26 June*

- Maria Bueno beats Dorothy Hard for Women's Wimbledon singles final   *4 July*

- Yorkshire win Cricket County Championship   *1 September*

- Stirling Moss wins 257 mile long Italian Grand Prix in a rear-engined Coventry Climax   *13 September*

- Jockey Manny Mercer killed after falling from his horse at Ascot   *26 September*

1959
Happenings 3

June *continued*
- Canada: The Queen and President Dwight D Eisenhower open the St Lawrence Seaway.
- Liberace wins £8,000 damages from Daily Mirror after columnist Cassandra suggests he was a homosexual

July
- Fidel Castro becomes Cuban President.
- Average British male manual worker earns £13 2s 11d per week.
- House of Fraser launches take-over bid for Harrods.

August
- Alex Issigonis's new revolutionary cars are introduced. These are the Austin Seven and the Morris Mini-Minor.
- Barclays bank becomes the first bank to use a computer for its branch accounts.
- 800 year old Les Halles market area to be demolished as it is costly and inefficient.
- The Queen is expecting her 3rd child who will become Prince Andrew.

September
- USSR rocket Lunik II is launched at the moon.

- 47 coal miners trapped in pit at Aughengeich Colliery near Glasgow.
- Opera singer Maria Callas denies liaison with Aristotle Onassis after she leaves her husband.
- Ceylon PM Solomon Bandaranaike dies after assassination attempt by a Buddhist monk two days earlier.

October
- Conservatives under the leadership of Harold Macmillan win General Election with a majority of 107 over the Labour Party.
- Survey shows that 1/3rd of 15 year old UK boys smoke cigarettes.
- First ever photographs of the dark side of the moon.

November
- M1 motorway opened.
- Belgium flies in first troops to quell disturbances in Belgian Congo.
- European Free Trade Association agreement signed between Austria, Britain, Denmark, Norway, Portugal, Sweden and Switzerland.

December
- Antarctica designated a science reserve by 12 countries.
- 300 people die after dam collapses and then washes away part of the town of Frejus in the French Riviera.
- US satellite returns a monkey who travelled 55 miles out into space.

- Archbishop Makarios elected first President of Cyprus.
- Hawker Siddeley and de Havilland aircraft companies to merge.

TROLLEYBUS CLOSURES IN 1959

- Brighton, Hove & District 24 March 1959
- Hastings 31 May 1959

TRAM CLOSURES IN 1959

- Leeds 7 November 1959

Index

Introduction   3

BMMO Types

C1	4
C2	7,8
C3	10,12
C5	5,6,10
CM5T	5,6
CVA6	16
D1	34
D5	17,34
D5b	25,30,38
D7	2,13,16,29
D9	16
S10	2,14,19,42
S12	26
S13	41,42
S14	5,6,13,15,17, 20,22,29,39
S15	5,20,29,31,32
S6	13,15,18,22,43
S8	14,15,16,20,37
S9	23
SOS Fedd	23,24,26,32
SOS ONC	4,7,10,15
Ex-London Transport RT	20

Fleet Numbers

2123	13
2141	24
2228	13
2231	30
2243	27
2272	10
2277	4
2286	7
2291	4
2336	22,23
2343	32
2346	23
2361	26
2372	24
2427	33
3001	43
3006	13
3010	18
3075	22
3082	15
3102	35
3109	18
3111	18
3126	44
3217	20
3229	16
3249	37
3255	15
3291	14
3304	9
3307	10
3338	9
3349	8
3356	7
3364	23
3471	34
3483	17
3566	35
3599	2
3633	19
3676	42
3731	14
3757	26
3784	38
3788	25
3911	41,42
4012	36
4026	30
4100	29
4124	2
4201	11
4219	12
4232	10
4238	11
4255	17
4332	15
4371	29
4573	22
4584	13
4603	32
4609	31
4621	29
4707	20,21
4708	39
4722	6
4748	40
4757	13
4773	16
4793	10
4809	5,6
4814	5
4843	33
4844	45
4847	45

Places

Aberystwyth	12
Acocks Green	22,37
Axbridge	9
Banbury	4,40
Barston	22
Bawtry	8
Bearwood	24,29,32,34,37
Beoley	31
Bescot	2
Birmingham	2,3,4,5,6,8,13, 14,16,22,23,24,25, 26,27,29,30,31,32,, 33,37,38
Birmingham New Street	2
Black & White Motorways	7
Blackheath	29,34
Blackpool	12
Bordesley	24
Bourneheath	37
Bournemouth	4,12
Bridgnorth	41
Brockhampton	18
Bromsgrove	32,37
Burton	26,29
Carlyle Road Works	5
Cheddar	9
Cheltenham	7,21
Chipping Campden	39
Coalbrookdale	2
Coleshill	30
Coventry	11,14,16,22,23,46
Cradley Heath	35
Cubbington	16
Curdworth	23
Digbeth Coach Station	4,5
Drayton Manor Park	23
Dudley	3,22,23,29,32,35,36
Emscote	13
Erdington	23
Evesham	17,20,38,39
Gaddesby	43
Gloucester	9
Great Bridge	35
Great North Road	8
Great Yarmouth	10,12
Gretna Green	7
Hagley Road	32
Hall Green	22,24,30
Hay-on-wye	42
Henley-in-arden	16
Hereford	18,42
High Park Estate	18
Ironbridge	42
Ironbridge	2,42
Kemp & Shaw	17,33,45
Kidderminster	2
Kings Heath	31
Kingswinford	36
Knowle	22,30
Ladywood	29
Langley	32
Ledbury	42
Leicester	2,7,17,33,43,45
Leicester City F.C.	7
Leominster	42
Lichfield	26
Llandudno	12
Lodge Road	29
London	3,5,6,8,11,14,20
London Bridge Station	11
Londonderry	32
Loughborough	44
M45 Motorway	6
Marston Green	37
Melton Mowbray	43
Monkspath	24
Netherton	35
New Milverton	14
Northampton	11
Norton Estate	18
Nuneaton	20
Oldbury	25,26,29,32,34
Old Hill	35
Olton	37
Oxford	13
Pensnett	36
Pershore	17
Pool Meadow	16
Portway	34,38
Priory Estate	35
Quinton	33
Reasby	43
Redditch	31
Rednal	32
Rosebery Street Depot	29
Ross-on-wye	18,42
Rounds Green	34
Rowley Regis	29
Rugby	3,5,14
Saltley Road	30
Selly Oak	32
Shipston-on-stour	39
Shirley	16,24,36
Shrewsbury	2,45
Skegness	12
Smethwick	33
Smethwick	29,33
Solihull	22,24,30,37
Solihull Lodge	37,38
South Wigston	17
Spa, Leamington	13,14,15
Stoneleigh	16
Stourbridge	18
Stratford-upon-avon	4,16
Streetley	2
Sutton Coldfield	23,26
Sutton Park	2
Tamworth	23
Tipton	35
Torquay	12
Vale Of Evesham	17
Victoria Coach Station	6
Wall Heath	36
Walsall	2
Warwick	2,13,14,15,22
Watford	3,5
Wednesbury	35
Wellesbourne	15
Wellington	2,19,41
Weston-super-mare	12
Worcester	17,23,29,42
Wylde Green	23
Wythall	37

Rivers

River Blythe	22
River Cole	30
River Idle	8
River Severn	42

THE END